United States Government Accountability Office

Report to Congressional Committees

I0411709

September 2014

DEFENSE INFRASTRUCTURE

DOD Needs to Improve Its Efforts to Identify Unutilized and Underutilized Facilities

GAO-14-538

Highlights

Highlights of GAO-14-538, a report to
congressional committees

DEFENSE INFRASTRUCTURE

DOD Needs to Improve Its Efforts to Identify Unutilized and Underutilized Facilities

Why GAO Did This Study

GAO has designated DOD's Support Infrastructure Management as a high-risk area in part due to challenges DOD faces in reducing excess infrastructure. DOD manages a global real property portfolio of over 557,000 facilities DOD estimates to be valued at about $828 billion as of September 30, 2012. In September 2011, GAO found that DOD was limited in its ability to reduce excess inventory because OSD did not maintain accurate and complete data on the utilization of its facilities in its Real Property Assets Database.

House Report 113-102 mandated GAO to review DOD efforts to improve these data. This report examines the extent to which OSD has (1) improved the completeness and accuracy of facility-utilization data in its Real Property Assets Database and the military departments' use of data to identify consolidation opportunities, and (2) a strategic plan to manage DOD's real property efficiently and to facilitate the identification of unutilized and underutilized facilities. GAO analyzed OSD's real property data from fiscal years 2010 through 2013, visited 11 active DOD installations from the four services to reflect those with high numbers of buildings, and interviewed officials. While not generalizable, the interviews provided perspectives about facility utilization.

What GAO Recommends

GAO recommends that OSD establish a strategic plan to identify unutilized and underutilized facilities. In written comments on a draft of the report, DOD concurred with the recommendation.

View GAO-14-538. For more information, contact Brian J. Lepore at (202) 512-4523 or leporeb@gao.gov

What GAO Found

The Office of the Secretary of Defense (OSD) has made some improvements, but OSD's utilization data continue to be incomplete and inaccurate; and data limitations affect the military departments' use of their databases to identify consolidation opportunities. GAO's analysis found that the percentage of total real property assets with a reported utilization rate in OSD's Real Property Assets Database increased from 46 to 53 percent over the past 4 fiscal years. OSD made some improvements in addressing inaccuracies in the utilization rates in its real property records, such as correcting records for those facilities reported with a utilization rate greater than 100 percent. The military departments use databases to a certain degree to identify opportunities to consolidate facilities, but primarily only in response to specific events, such as requests for space. Officials at all 11 installations GAO visited stated that inaccurate and incomplete data in the departments' databases limited opportunities to identify these opportunities. In September 2011, GAO recommended that the Department of Defense (DOD) develop and implement a methodology for calculating and recording utilization data, and modify processes to update and verify the accuracy of reported data. OSD partially concurred because it stated that it had some actions already underway to address the recommendation. However, at that time, OSD did not specify what actions it had undertaken. Moreover, the recommendation has not yet been fully implemented. Fully implementing GAO's recommendation would help provide reasonable assurance that the utilization data are complete and accurate and better position the department to use the databases to identify consolidation opportunities.

OSD does not have a strategic plan, with goals and metrics, to manage DOD's real property efficiently and facilitate identifying opportunities for consolidating unutilized or underutilized facilities. According to a DOD directive, it is DOD policy that DOD real property shall be managed to promote the most efficient and economic use of DOD real property assets, and in the most economical manner consistent with defense requirements. However, OSD officials stated that there is currently no OSD strategic plan to manage DOD's real property nor established department-wide goals, strategies to achieve the goals, or metrics to gauge progress for how it intends to manage its real property in the most efficient manner. Such goals could focus on correcting inaccurate and incomplete facility utilization data to provide better visibility on the status of facilities and to identify opportunities for consolidating unutilized or underutilized facilities and reducing operations and maintenance costs. GAO's prior work has shown that organizations need sound strategic planning to identify and achieve long-range goals and objectives. Without a strategic plan, it will be difficult for OSD to effectively manage its facilities and utilize them efficiently.

Contents

Abbreviations

DOD   Department of Defense
OMB   Office of Management and Budget
OSD   Office of the Secretary of Defense

September 8, 2014

Congressional Committees

Since 1997, we have designated the Department of Defense's (DOD) Support Infrastructure Management as a high-risk area, in part due to the challenges DOD faces in reducing excess and obsolete infrastructure.[1] DOD manages a global real property portfolio that, according to DOD, as of the end of fiscal year 2012 consisted of more than 557,000 facilities (buildings, structures, and linear structures[2]), located on over 5,000 sites worldwide, covering more than 27.7 million acres, and with a value of approximately $828 billion.[3] The operation and maintenance of unutilized and underutilized facilities consumes valuable resources that could be eliminated from DOD's budget or used by DOD for other purposes.

We found in September 2011 that DOD was limited in its ability to reduce excess inventory because DOD did not maintain accurate and complete data regarding the utilization of its facilities.[4] For example, we found that the Office of the Secretary of Defense's (OSD) Real Property Assets Database—a compilation of the military departments' real property assets inventory—showed facility utilization data for less than half of DOD's total inventory, and these data often were incomplete or did not reflect the true usage rate of the facilities. For example, data for the Air Force showed a utilization rate of 0 percent for 22,563 buildings that were reported to be in

---

[1] GAO, *High-Risk Series: Defense Infrastructure*, GAO/HR-97-7 (Washington, D.C.: February 1997); *High-Risk Series: An Update*, GAO-11-278 (Washington, D.C.: February 2011); and *High-Risk Series: An Update*, GAO-13-283 (Washington D.C.: February 2013). The High-Risk Series focuses on government operations that we have identified as high risk because of their greater vulnerabilities to fraud, waste, abuse, and mismanagement, or the need for transformation to address economy, efficiency, or effectiveness challenges.

[2] A linear structure is a facility whose function requires that it traverse land (e.g., runway, road, rail line, pipeline, fence, pavement, electrical distribution line) and is reported by a linear unit of measure.

[3] Department of Defense, Deputy Under Secretary of Defense for Installations and Environment, *Base Structure Report Fiscal Year 2013 Baseline, A Summary of DOD's Real Property Inventory* as of September 30, 2012, which were the most-recent data available at the time of our review.

[4] GAO, *Excess Facilities: DOD Needs More Complete Information and a Strategy to Guide Its Future Disposal Efforts*, GAO-11-814 (Washington, D.C.: Sept. 19, 2011).

an active status. We also found that DOD's plans to eliminate excess facilities in the future were unclear, as were its plans for taking into account external factors, such as management of historical-preservation requirements and environmental restrictions, which affect the disposal of long-standing excess facilities that were identified before fiscal year 2008. For example, we found that DOD had not defined the strategies and measures it intended to employ to eliminate excess facilities on its installations. We concluded that, to the extent that DOD has identified unutilized and underutilized facilities, additional cost savings might be realized through the consolidation or disposal of such real property inventory. We made two recommendations to DOD, with which it partially concurred, related to improving its data and developing strategies and measures to enhance the management of its facilities, as discussed later in this report.

House Report 113-102, accompanying a bill for the National Defense Authorization Act for Fiscal Year 2014,[5] mandated GAO to report to the congressional defense committees on DOD's efforts to improve the accuracy of its real property database and the effect of those efforts on DOD's consolidation activities. This report addresses the extent to which (1) OSD has improved the completeness and accuracy of facility utilization data in its Real Property Assets Database, and the military departments use the data contained in their respective real property inventory databases to identify potential consolidation opportunities; and (2) OSD has a strategic plan to manage DOD's real property efficiently and to facilitate the identification of unutilized and underutilized facilities.

To determine the extent to which OSD has improved the completeness and accuracy of facility utilization data in its Real Property Assets Database and the military departments use the data contained in their respective real property inventory databases to identify potential consolidation opportunities, we obtained selected data fields containing the military departments' real property records from OSD's Real Property Assets Database. We selected the same data fields we had used as part of our methodology and analysis for our September 2011 report.[6]

---

[5]Pub. L. No. 113-66 (2013).

[6]Specifically, we analyzed the following three data fields: (1) the utilization rate; (2) the status, and (3) the property description. For more information about the methodology used for our September 2011 report, see GAO-11-814.

Specifically, we analyzed the utilization-rate data fields for fiscal years 2010 through 2013—the most recent full year available at the time of this review—to determine whether more complete utilization-rate data had been entered since our previous review of the fiscal year 2010 data. We assessed the reliability of DOD's real property inventory data by (1) performing electronic testing for obvious errors in accuracy and completeness, (2) reviewing existing information about the data and the system that produced them, and (3) interviewing agency officials knowledgeable about the data. We determined that the data were sufficiently reliable to assess the trends of the utilization data reported in OSD's Real Property Assets Database for fiscal years 2010 through 2013. We also reviewed our prior work on excess and underutilized real property to understand issues previously identified with real property management. We gathered and analyzed documentation, such as a DOD directive and instructions as well as military-department regulations, reflecting OSD's and the military departments' management of real property and how OSD used the data contained in its Real Property Assets Database to identify unutilized or underutilized facilities or potential consolidation opportunities. We interviewed officials in the Office of the Under Secretary of Defense for Installations and Environment; each of the three military departments, which include the four military services; and the military service installations we visited, and discussed their processes to manage real property. We selected 11 active military installations to visit to include installations from the four military services and to reflect those with high numbers of buildings.[7] While the results of our interviews and visits cannot be generalized to all installations, they provided perspectives on how installations manage their real property. Using OSD's Real Property Assets Database and the utilization-rate data fields discussed above, we used a fourth data field, which described the asset as "utilized," to determine inconsistencies between these data fields. Using these four criteria, we reviewed the real property records for the 11 installations we visited to identify the extent to which other consolidation opportunities, if any, may exist on the installations and potential inconsistencies and inaccuracies.

---

[7]For our methodology, we selected 11 active installations that each had at least 500 buildings on them as reported in *DOD's Base Structure Report Fiscal Year 2013 Baseline*. The selection included 3 Army, 3 Navy, 2 Marine Corps, and 3 U.S. Air Force installations or bases, which represented 5.4 percent of the 203 active installations and bases within the continental United States excluding the National Guard and the Reserves. For this report, we use the term "installation" to represent either an active military installation or base.

To determine the extent to which OSD has a strategic plan to manage DOD's real property efficiently and to facilitate the identification of unutilized and underutilized facilities, we obtained and analyzed documentation, such as the Office of the Deputy Under Secretary of Defense for Installations and Environment report, *2013 Accomplishments and 2014 Goals and Objectives*, a DOD directive and instructions, and military department regulations for the management of real property. We also reviewed OSD's Real Property Assets Database as of September 30, 2013—the most recent data available at the time of our review—to identify what facilities, if any, were reported as being unutilized or underutilized and ascertain how OSD implemented its policy and guidance to manage real property in the most economical manner, consistent with defense requirements. We discussed the policies and guidance used in managing these facilities with officials in the Office of the Under Secretary of Defense for Installations & Environment, and compared OSD's efforts and guidance to DOD instructions for real property management and the results-oriented management framework as a best practice for strategic planning.[8] Further details on our scope and methodology can be found in appendix I.

We conducted this performance audit from July 2013 to September 2014 in accordance with generally accepted government auditing standards. Those standards require that we plan and perform the audit to obtain sufficient, appropriate evidence to provide a reasonable basis for our findings and conclusions based on our audit objectives. We believe that the evidence obtained provides a reasonable basis for our findings and conclusions based on our audit objectives.

---

[8]Department of Defense Directive 4165.06, *Real Property* (Oct. 13, 2004, certified current Nov. 18, 2008); Department of Defense Instruction 4165.70, *Real Property Management* (Apr. 6, 2005); and Department of Defense Instruction 4165.14, *Real Property Inventory (RPI) and Forecasting* (Jan. 17, 2014). See, for example, GAO, *Managing for Results: Critical Issues for Improving Federal Agencies' Strategic Plans*, GAO/GGD-97-180 (Washington, D.C.: Sept. 16, 1997); *Major Management Challenges and Program Risks: A Governmentwide Perspective*, GAO-03-95 (Washington, D.C.: January 2003); and *Military Transformation: Clear Leadership, Accountability, and Management Tools Are Needed to Enhance DOD's Efforts to Transform Military Capabilities*, GAO-05-70 (Washington, D.C.: Dec. 17, 2004). These reports described that strategic plans are the starting point and basic underpinning for results-oriented management, a results-oriented management framework can help the federal government operate effectively, and successful organizations in both the public and private sectors use results-oriented management tools to help achieve desired program outcomes. One of the reports identified the framework that includes various management tools, such as long-term goals, strategies to be used, performance goals, and performance measures, among others. To determine these best practices, we found studies by several organizations, including us, that show that results-oriented management tools or principles, derived from the Government Performance and Results Act of 1993, provide agencies with a management framework for effectively implementing and managing programs and shift program management focus from measuring program activities and processes to measuring program outcomes. See GAO, *Results-Oriented Government: GPRA Has Established a Solid Foundation for Achieving Greater Results*, GAO-04-38 (Washington, D.C.: Mar. 10, 2004); *Managing For Results: Enhancing Agency Use of Performance Information for Management Decision Making*, GAO-05-927 (Washington, D.C.: Sept. 9, 2005); and *Results-Oriented Management: Strengthening Key Practices at FEMA and Interior Could Promote Greater Use of Performance Information*, GAO-09-676 (Washington, D.C.: Aug. 17, 2009) for additional details on the methodology used to determine these best practices.

Background

DOD's and Military Departments' Guidance and Responsibilities for Managing Real Property

DOD's Real Property Management Program is governed by statute[9] and DOD regulations, directives, and instructions that establish real property accountability and financial reporting requirements. These laws, regulations, directives, and instructions—a selection of which are discussed below—require DOD and the military departments to maintain a number of data elements about their facilities to help ensure efficient property management and thus help identify potential facility consolidation opportunities.

Three DOD documents—DOD Directive 4165.06,[10] DOD Instruction 4165.14,[11] and DOD Instruction 4165.70[12]—assign responsibilities for managing DOD's real property inventory to a number of organizations, including the Under Secretary of Defense for Acquisition, Technology and Logistics and the military departments. Specifically, the directive assigns overall responsibility and oversight of DOD real property to the Under Secretary of Defense for Acquisition, Technology and Logistics, but assigns specific responsibilities to the Secretaries of the three military departments[13] for real property management, including implementing policies and programs to acquire, manage, and dispose of real property. Accordingly, each of the military departments has developed its own procedures and guidance for managing its infrastructure. Some of the key guidance used by the military departments for managing real property

---

[9]Section 2721 of Title 10 of the United States Code directs the Secretary of Defense to prescribe regulations to, among other things, have the records of fixed property of the military departments maintained on a quantitative and monetary basis, to the extent practicable.

[10]Department of Defense Directive 4165.06, *Real Property* (Oct. 13, 2004, certified current Nov.18, 2008).

[11]Department of Defense Instruction 4165.14, *Real Property Inventory (RPI) and Forecasting* (Jan. 17, 2014).

[12]Department of Defense Instruction 4165.70, *Real Property Management* (Apr. 6, 2005).

[13]The three military departments are headed, respectively, by the Secretary of the Army, the Secretary of the Navy (for the Navy and the Marine Corps), and the Secretary of the Air Force. In addition, for certain functions related to real property management of the Pentagon Reservation, Washington Headquarters Services is considered a military department and its Director the secretary thereof as defined in DOD Instruction 4165.70, *Real Property Management*, (Apr. 6, 2005).

includes Army Regulation 405-70; the Naval Facilities Engineering Command P-78; and Air Force Policy Directive 32-10.[14] The guidance requires, among other things, that real property records be accurate and be managed efficiently and economically. It also requires the military departments to maintain a complete and accurate real property inventory with up-to-date information, to annually certify that the real property inventory has been reconciled, and to ensure that all real property holdings under the military departments' control are being used to the maximum extent possible. Appendix II describes some of the guidance from DOD and the military departments and includes excerpts of the related requirements to manage real property.

In managing the real property under their control, the military departments are responsible for implementing real property policies and programs to, among other things, hold or make plans to obtain the land and facilities they need for their own missions and for other DOD components' missions that are supported by the military departments' real property. Additionally, the military departments are required to (1) budget for and financially manage so as to meet their own real property requirements; (2) accurately inventory and account for their land and facilities; and (3) maintain a program monitoring the use of real property to ensure that all holdings under their control are being used to the maximum extent possible consistent with both peacetime and mobilization requirements.

The military departments' processes for managing and monitoring the utilization of facilities generally occur at the installation level. According to OSD guidance, inventories are to be conducted every 5 years except for those real property assets designated as historic, which are to be reviewed and physically inventoried every 3 years. According to DOD Instruction 4165.70, the military departments' real property administrators are accountable for maintaining a current inventory count of the military departments' facilities and up-to-date information regarding, among other things, the status, condition, utilization, present value, and remaining useful life of each real property asset.[15] Inventory counts and associated

---

[14]Army Regulation 405-70, *Utilization of Real Property* (May 12, 2006); Naval Facilities Engineering Command (NAVFAC) P-78, *Real Property Inventory (RPI) Procedures Manual* (July 2008); Air Force Policy Directive 32-10, *Installations and Facilities* (Mar. 4, 2010).

[15]Department of Defense Instruction 4165.70, *Real Property Management* (Apr. 6, 2005) and DOD Instruction 4165.14, *Real Property Inventory (RPI) and Forecasting* (Jan. 17, 2014).

information should be current as of the last day of each fiscal year. When DOD's real property is no longer needed for current or projected defense requirements, it is DOD's policy to dispose of it. In addition, DOD Instruction 4165.70 requires the military departments to periodically review their real property holdings, both land and facilities, to identify unneeded and underused property.

The three military departments maintain a number of real property databases that are to be used to manage real property assets for the Army, Navy, Marine Corps, and the Air Force as shown in table 1.

Table 1: Military Department Databases Used to Manage Real Property

Department	Name of database
Army	General Fund Enterprise Business System
	Real Property Planning and Analysis System
	Real Estate Management Information System
	Rental Facilities Management Information System
	Headquarters Installation Information System
Navy (comprising the Navy and Marine Corps)	Shore Facilities Planning System
	Internet Navy Facilities Assets Data Store
Air Force	Automated Civil Engineer System-Real Property
	S-File Installation Tool

Source: GAO review of military department data. | GAO-14-538

OSD's Real Property Portfolio and Database

OSD's Base Structure Report Fiscal Year 2013 Baseline (OSD's Base Structure Report) is a summary of DOD's real property inventory and a "snapshot" of DOD's real property data collected as of September 30, 2012, and serves as the beginning balance for fiscal year 2013.[16] The report identifies DOD's real property assets, including buildings, structures, and linear structures, worldwide. Table 2 shows the total assets, percentages, and plant replacement values[17] of real property assets for each of the military departments and the Washington Headquarters Services.

---

[16]This was the most recent *Base Structure Report* available at the time of our review.

[17]The plant replacement value represents the calculated cost to replace the current physical plant (facilities and supporting infrastructure) using today's construction costs (labor and materials) and standards (methodologies and codes).

Table 2: DOD's Real Property Portfolio as of September 30, 2012

Military service	Number of assets	Percentage of total assets per military service	Plant replacement value (dollars in billions)
Army	261,622	47%	$310.28
Navy	113,668	20	203.11
Marine Corps	46,134	8	60.40
Air Force	134,979	24	247.12
Washington Headquarters Services	773	1	7.02
Total	**557,176**	**100%**	**$827.93**

Source: Office of the Secretary of Defense (OSD). | GAO-14-538

Note: Data are from *OSD's Base Structure Report Fiscal Year 2013 Baseline*.

OSD compiles and maintains the department's real property assets inventory in a single database, called the Real Property Assets Database. OSD's Real Property Assets Database contains specific reporting data on the military departments' real property records and is considered the single authoritative source for all DOD real property inventory. OSD's objectives for the Real Property Assets Database are to comply with current DOD business architecture, support the DOD standardized real property requirements, and implement DOD Instruction 4165.14: *Real Property Inventory and Forecasting*. The Real Property Assets Database is the source used for OSD's annual real property reporting that includes the Federal Real Property Profile report[18] and OSD's *Base Structure Report*. OSD's *Base Structure Report* is a snapshot of real property assets as of September 30 of the previous fiscal year and serves as the baseline for each contemporaneous fiscal year. It is a consolidated summary of the three military departments' real property inventory data, submitted annually. The three military departments' real property inventory records, which are the source for compiling DOD's real property records on an annual basis, are uploaded to OSD's Real Property Assets

---

[18]Federal agencies are required to annually list and describe real property assets under their jurisdiction, custody, or control to the Director of the Office of Management and Budget (OMB) and the Administrator of the General Services Administration through the Federal Real Property Profile. The Federal Real Property Council's guidance requires that DOD and other federal agencies annually report utilization information for five categories of buildings—(1) offices, (2) warehouses, (3) hospitals, (4) laboratories, and (5) housing (family housing, dormitories, or barracks)—as part of the agencies' data submissions for the Federal Real Property Profile report.

Database. Additionally, the Secretaries of the military departments are to certify annually that the real property inventory records have been reconciled.

Our Prior Work on DOD's Real Property Assets Database

In September 2011,[19] we found that as of September 30, 2010, DOD's Real Property Assets Database reported utilization data for fewer than half of DOD's total inventory of facilities and that much of the data were outdated and did not reflect the true usage of the structures. OSD stated at the time that utilization data in its database did not cover the full DOD inventory because the primary focus of the department's efforts to collect and record such data had been in response to reporting requirements from the Federal Real Property Council, which requires annual reports on utilization of five categories of buildings for the Federal Real Property Profile. However, OSD annually reports all of its real property in its *Base Structure Report*. Further, we found that when utilization-rate data were recorded in OSD's database, the recorded entry often did not reflect the true usage of the facilities. For example, we found that in fiscal year 2010 the real property data for the Air Force reported a utilization rate of 0 percent for 22,563 buildings that were reported to be in an active status. As a result, we recommended that the Secretary of Defense direct the Deputy Under Secretary of Defense for Installations and Environment to (1) develop and implement a methodology for calculating and recording utilization data for all types of facilities and to modify their processes for updating and verifying the accuracy of reported utilization data to reflect a facility's true status and (2) develop strategies and measures to enhance the management of DOD's excess facilities after the current demolition program ends, taking into account external factors that might affect future disposal efforts. OSD partially concurred with our first recommendation because it stated that it had some actions already underway to address the recommendation. However, at that time, OSD did not specify what actions it had undertaken to date or the time frames for completing efforts to improve the collection and reporting of utilization data. DOD concurred with our second recommendation, but did not provide any details or specific time frames for efforts to address it. As of June 2014, according to OSD officials, they have not fully implemented these two recommendations.

---

[19]GAO-11-814.

In the update to our High-Risk Series,[20] we found that DOD faced challenges in reducing excess and obsolete infrastructure, sustaining facilities, and achieving cost savings and efficiencies in base support by eliminating duplication of support services where bases are in close proximity to or adjacent to one another. We concluded that DOD's progress on its long-term demolition plans beyond fiscal year 2013 remains unclear, and that DOD at that time stated that it continued to have significant excess capacity relative to the planned force structure. Further, we concluded that DOD is limited in its ability to identify potentially excess facilities because it does not maintain complete and accurate data concerning the utilization of its facilities as well as long-standing problems in managing federal real property.

Results-Oriented Management Framework Approach

Our body of work on results-oriented management has shown that successful organizations in both the public and private sectors use results-oriented management tools to help achieve desired program outcomes.[21] These tools, or principles, derived from the Government Performance and Results Act (GPRA) of 1993,[22] provide agencies with a management framework for effectively implementing and managing programs and shift program-management focus from measuring program activities and processes to measuring program outcomes. The framework can include various management tools, such as long-term goals, performance goals, and performance measures, which can assist agencies in measuring performance and reporting results. Our prior work has also shown that organizations need effective strategic management planning in order to identify and achieve long-term goals. We have identified key elements that should be incorporated into strategic plans to

---

[20]GAO-13-283.

[21]See, for example, GAO-05-70.

[22]Pub. L. No. 103-62 (1993). Although GPRA's requirements apply at the agency level, based on our review of related GAO products, OMB guidance, and studies by the National Academy of Public Administration and the Urban Institute, we have previously reported that these requirements can serve as leading practices in lower levels within an organization, such as with individual programs or initiatives. See GAO, *Pipeline Safety: Management of the Office of Pipeline Safety's Enforcement Program Needs Further Strengthening*, GAO-04-801 (Washington, D.C.: July, 2004). GAO/GGD-97-180; GAO-05-70; *Defense Management: Fully Developed Management Framework Needed to Guide Air Force Future Total Force Efforts*, GAO-06-232 (Washington, D.C.: Jan. 31, 2006); and GAO-09-676.

help establish a comprehensive, results-oriented management framework for programs within DOD.[23]

Further our prior body of work has also shown that organizations conducting strategic planning need to develop a comprehensive, results-oriented management framework to remain operationally effective, efficient, and capable of meeting future requirements.[24] A results-oriented management framework provides an approach whereby program effectiveness is measured in terms of outcome metrics. Approaches to such planning vary according to agency-specific needs and missions; however, irrespective of the context in which planning is done, our prior work has shown that such a strategic plan should contain the following seven critical elements: (1) a comprehensive mission statement; (2) long-term goals; (3) strategies to achieve the goals; (4) use of metrics to gauge progress; (5) identification of key external factors that could affect the achievement of the goals; (6) a discussion of how program evaluations will be used; and (7) stakeholder involvement in developing the plan.[25]

---

[23]See, for example, GAO, *Depot Maintenance: Improved Strategic Planning Needed to Ensure That Army and Marine Corps Depots Can Meet Future Maintenance Requirements*, GAO-09-865 (Washington, D.C.: Sept. 17, 2009); *Depot Maintenance: Improved Strategic Planning Needed to Ensure That Air Force Depots Can Meet Future Maintenance Requirements*, GAO-10-526 (Washington, D.C.: May 14, 2010); and *Depot Maintenance: Improved Strategic Planning Needed to Ensure That Navy Depots Can Meet Future Maintenance Requirements*, GAO-10-585 (Washington, D.C.: June 11, 2010).

[24]GAO-05-70 and GAO-09-676.

[25]See, for example, GAO-09-865; GAO-10-526; and GAO-10-585.

OSD Has Made Some Improvements, but Facility Utilization Data Continue to Be Incomplete and Inaccurate; Data Limitations Affect Use of Departments' Databases to Identify Consolidation Opportunities

OSD Has Made Some Improvements, but Facility Utilization Data Continue to Be Incomplete and Inaccurate

In our analysis of OSD's Real Property Assets Database over the past 4 fiscal years, we found that although the department has made some progress in improving its real property records, OSD continued to collect incomplete utilization data for its real property assets. Specifically, we found that OSD's methodology for calculating and recording utilization data has not changed since our September 2011 report and the data continue to be incomplete and not encompass all of DOD's assets. OSD guidance requires that utilization rates be included for all categories of its real property asset records. The percentage of total real property assets with a reported utilization rate increased from 46 percent to 53 percent over the past 4 fiscal years, as shown in table 3.

Table 3: Percentage of DOD Total Real Property Assets with a Reported Utilization Rate for Fiscal Years 2010 through 2013

Fiscal year	DOD's real property assets	Total real property assets with a reported utilization rate	Percentage of total real property assets with a reported utilization rate	Total real property assets with no reported utilization rate	Percentage of total real property assets with no reported utilization rate
2010	521,500	238,498	46%	283,002	54%
2011	508,950	222,829	44	286,121	56
2012	520,371	234,485	45	285,886	55
2013	524,189	278,908	53	245,281	47

Source: GAO's analysis of DOD data. | GAO-14-538

Note: Data are from the Office of the Secretary of Defense's (OSD) Real Property Assets Database.

GAO-14-538 Defense Infrastructure

For example, as of September 30, 2013, we found that facility utilization data were missing for 245,281 of DOD's 524,189[26] assets—that is, about 47 percent of its total real property assets. Although the percentage of facilities not reporting any utilization rate decreased since 2011, OSD's fiscal year 2013 database still reflects that almost half of DOD's total real property assets records do not reflect a utilization rate.

Further, related to accuracy of the data, we found a number of real property assets reporting a zero utilization rate, which may indicate either inaccurate records or some type of a consolidation opportunity. We used three data fields to determine whether a facility's utilization was consistently reported in OSD's Real Property Assets Database. Specifically, we used the following three criteria—a utilization rate reported as "zero" (indicating the facility was not being utilized), a status reported as "active" (indicating the facility was being utilized), and the type of asset described as a "building." We found that as of September 30, 2013, OSD reported 7,596 buildings across the four military services with inconsistent or inaccurate reported utilization, as shown in table 4.[27]

Table 4: Number of Facilities with a Reported Utilization Rate of Zero, Active Status, and Real Property Described as a Building as of Fiscal Year End, September 30, 2010, through September 30, 2013

Fiscal year	Total	Army	Navy	Marine Corps	Air Force
2010	**23,918**	1,316	21	18	22,563
2011	**2,313**	1,373	19	20	901
2012	**1,501**	197	9	12	1,283
2013	**7,596**	6,391	13	18	1,174

Source: GAO's analysis of DOD data. | GAO-14-538

Note: Data are from the Office of the Secretary of Defense's (OSD) Real Property Assets Database.

---

[26]The difference between the 557,176 buildings, structures, and linear structures reported in the *Base Structure Report Fiscal Year 2013 Baseline* and the data OSD provided to us within its Real Property Assets Database is due to OSD's having excluded from the database some land easements, private holdings, and privatized housing.

[27]We further analyzed the 7,596 facilities to determine the number of facilities that were part of the five specific categories of buildings for the Federal Real Property Profile and found that the Air Force and Army had 521 and 1,771 respectively. The Marine Corps and Navy did not have any facilities that were part of the five categories of buildings for the Federal Real Property Profile.

We then assessed these facilities and found that 30 percent (2,255 of the 7,596 facilities) were also described as "utilized" in the Real Property Assets Database. Having a utilization rate of zero and being in an active status and described as utilized shows potential inconsistencies or inaccuracies in the data.

We analyzed the inconsistencies across the four services and found the following:

- The Army reported 6,391 real property records with a zero utilization rate, but 1,734 (about 27 percent) of those buildings were described as utilized; the remainder of the Army's records noted 37 buildings (about 0.01 percent) described as underutilized; and 4,620 (about 72 percent) of those buildings had no utilization description.[28]
- The Navy's 13 buildings and the Marine Corps' 18 buildings that were reported with a zero utilization rate had no utilization description.
- Of the Air Force's 1,174 buildings reported with a zero utilization rate, 521 (about 44 percent) were described as utilized and 653 (about 56 percent) had no utilization description.

Our analysis also showed that OSD has made some improvements in addressing some other inaccuracies in the utilization rates in its real property records. For example, we found that OSD corrected its real property records for those reported with a utilization rate greater than 100 percent. Specifically, our analysis showed that OSD had previously reported real property records of 2,270; 2,093; and 999, in fiscal years 2010, 2011, and 2012, respectively, with a utilization rate greater than 100 percent. In fiscal year 2013, OSD had addressed this inaccuracy and reported no real property records with a utilization rate greater than 100 percent.

As another example, according to OSD's real property inventory data element dictionary, the utilization rate for its real property records should be reported as a whole number from 0 percent to 100 percent. Our analysis found that, since fiscal year 2010, OSD has been making progress in addressing the utilization rates that were not reported as

---

[28]According to OSD and Army officials, conversion issues occurred when the Army converted its real property records to its General Fund Enterprise Business System, and many of the Army's building utilization rates were erroneously changed to zero. According to OSD and Army officials, some of the building utilization rate data inaccuracies may be attributable to that conversion issue.

whole numbers and that, overall, the total number of real property records in OSD's Real Property Assets Database reporting a utilization rate that is not a whole number has steadily decreased over the past 4 fiscal years.[29]

Incomplete and Inaccurate Utilization Data Limit Use of Military Departments' Databases to Identify Consolidation Opportunities

As with our analysis of OSD's Real Property Assets Database, we found that the military departments do not collect and maintain accurate real property records in their respective databases, which limits the use of the databases as a tool to identify consolidation opportunities. We found, first, that at all 11 of the military service installations we visited, according to the installation officials, the utilization data are not systematically updated, but instead are updated when (1) there is a request for space; (2) a facility is consolidated or remodeled; (3) an area is being reviewed for potential military construction projects; (4) there may be a transfer of personnel at the installation; or (5) there is a periodic review of their real property holdings, both land and facilities, to identify unneeded and underused property.[30] Real property officials at all 11 of the military service installations we visited told us that evaluating the utilization of facilities requires physical inspections to verify and validate the accuracy of the utilization data within their real property inventory records. For example, according to Army Regulation 405-70, Army installations are required to perform an annual utilization survey and report findings of unused, underutilized, or excess real property.[31] The Navy and the Air Force do not have a similar requirement for annual utilization surveys. The Army regulation requires a report containing a list of unused or underutilized buildings by facility classes and category code, building number, total gross square feet, gross square feet available, type of

---

[29]Specifically, we found that OSD had reported 12,567; 7,456; 1,106; and 308 real property records with utilization rates that were not whole numbers since it included decimals for fiscal years 2010, 2011, 2012, and 2013, respectively. For example, within these rates, we found, respectively, 3,630; 3,298; and 2 real property records in OSD's Real Property Assets Database with a reported utilization rate that ranged from 0.01 percent through 0.99 percent from fiscal years 2010, 2011, 2012; we found none for 2013. Reporting thousands of utilization rates with decimals raised questions about whether the database had been portraying accurate utilization rates in cases where the rate is classified as a decimal when it should be reported as a whole number.

[30]DOD Instruction 4165.70 *Real Property Management* (Apr. 6, 2005), requires periodic reviews, but the instruction does not specify the time intervals for these reviews. However, Army Regulation 405-70, *Utilization of Real Property* (May 12, 2006), requires an annual utilization survey at Army installations.

[31]Army Regulation 405.70, *Utilization of Real Property* (May 12, 2006).

GAO-14-538 Defense Infrastructure

construction (permanent, semi-permanent, or temporary), and disposition. However, the real property officials at the three Army installations we visited told us that they had not completed the annual utilization surveys for their installations, because they did not have the manpower, the time to accomplish what they characterized as a time-consuming task on an annual basis, or the resources to pay a contractor to accomplish the task.

Secondly, we found during our discussions with service headquarters officials and visits to installations that those real property inventory records that are maintained in the military departments' authoritative real property inventory databases are not always accurate. For example:

- Army headquarters officials demonstrated a recently developed program called the Army's Quality Assurance Reporting Tool, which is used to detect inaccuracies within its real property inventory database at the installation level. In August 2013, Army officials showed us more than 45,000 errors of all types within the real property database for one of the installations we planned to visit.
- As of August 2013, Army headquarters officials provided us with a listing from one of their real property databases showing the dates when the installation facilities were reviewed. Based on our analysis of the list of facility review dates, we found significant anomalies. For example, we found that the list of facility review dates included such erroneous entries as the years 0012, 0013, 0201, 0212, 0213, 1012, 1776, 1777, 1839, 1855, 1886, 1887, 1888, 1889, 2020, 2030, 2114, 2114, 2201, and 3013. We told Army headquarters' officials about these particular facility review dates, and they responded that they would correct them. Table 5 below shows our analysis of the Army's review dates, building count, and percentage reviewed.[32]

---

[32]According to an OSD instruction, real property inventories are to be performed at a minimum every 5 years. DOD Instruction 4165.14, *Real Property Inventory (RPI) and Forecasting* (Jan. 17, 2014). We analyzed the review dates based on the 5-year inventory requirement.

Table 5: Army Facility Review Dates

Army Facility Review Dates	Building Count	Percentage Reviewed
Review dates prior to 2008	118,949	41%
Review dates 2008 through 2013	158,629	55
Review dates after 2013	10,331	4
Total	**287,909**	**100%**

Source: GAO analysis of Army data. | GAO-14-538

- In February 2014, Navy and Marine Corps headquarters' officials acknowledged that there are errors within the Internet Naval Facilities Assets Data Store database, which is the Navy's authoritative real property inventory database. For example, officials noted that some of the data, including the utilization rate, reported in the database may be inaccurate.

- At one of the naval sites we visited, officials stated that an audit within their naval region was conducted to verify the accuracy and completeness of the Navy's class-2 real property[33] inventory records in the Navy's authoritative real property inventory database. The Naval Audit Service performed an audit to verify that the Internet Navy Facility Assets Data Store was accurate and complete for the Navy's class-2 property inventory within one of the Navy's regions. Its report[34] notes that some of the data within this database were inaccurate and incomplete.

- At one of the Air Force bases we visited, an official provided a report by an Air Force Real Property Assertion Team[35] that conducted on-site visits to seven Air Force installations, which included this site, from June through July 2012. The report noted that internal control activities over manual real property processes were found to be ineffective, transactions lacked adequate supporting documentation,

---

[33]The Navy defines class-2 real property as improvements to land such as buildings, structures, ground improvement structures, utilities located within a building or structure, or built-in equipment.

[34]Department of the Navy, Naval Audit Service, *Navy's Real Property Inventory*, Audit Report N2014-0027 (June 9, 2014).

[35]In order to determine if established internal control procedures over the Air Forces' real property were operating effectively, a Real Property Assertion Team consisting of representatives from Headquarters Air Force, Civil Engineering, Asset Accountability and Optimization, the Deputy Assistant Secretary, Accounting and Financial Operations, and independent contractors was assembled.

and the authoritative real property inventory system provided inaccurate data and could not support audit readiness assertions over real property assets.

- Included in an Air Force Audit Agency report[36] at one of the installations we visited are five recommendations to develop and implement oversight procedures to validate the accuracy of Air Force's real property data.

Military installation-level officials at all 11 locations we visited told us that they use the departments' databases as a tool to help identify space requirements and potential consolidation opportunities; however, incomplete and inaccurate data limit the usefulness of the databases to do so. Specifically, according to these installation-level officials, because the utilization data currently contained in their databases are often missing, out of date, or inaccurate, the installations rely on physical verifications of facilities' utilization to identify consolidation opportunities. The installation-level officials stated that these physical verifications are performed as a result of requests for space or other common real property management processes, such as changes to mission and personnel at the installation. For example, at the 11 installations we visited, we found that consolidations had been performed in the past reactively in response to events, such as new or changing mission requirements, changes to force structure, or requests for facility space. Overall, the four military services use similar criteria and methodologies to address changes in mission requirements or requests for space at an installation. The installations' civil engineers, real property planners, and facility specialists analyze the installations' mission requirements and the space that is authorized to fulfill those missions in order to determine different potential courses of action for use of installation facilities. The installations are required by DOD Instruction 4165.14 to perform physical inventories every 5 years for real property and every 3 years for historical real property. Thus, according to the military installation-level officials, they generally complete 20 percent of the inventories each year, including verifying and correcting real property record data such as the utilization rate.

We analyzed OSD's Real Property Assets Database as of September 30, 2013, to determine whether some of the data fields could be used to

---

[36]Air Force Audit Agency, *Installation Report of Audit F2012-0029-FBM000*, Feb. 24, 2012.

identify potential consolidation opportunities.[37] In our analysis, we found, among the 11 locations we visited, that there were 12 real property assets or facilities that had data fields that indicated that they may have potential consolidation opportunities, which were located at 3 of the locations we visited.

At the first location, with 7 such facilities (including 4 office facilities), according to the real property officer, one of the office facilities was demolished in December 2013 and the real property record removed in January 2014. Another of the office facilities was demolished in November 2007, and the real property record should have been removed, yet it was present in DOD's September 30, 2013, real property records—reflecting an error that has been ongoing for more than 6 years. In addition, the real property officer noted that the remaining 2 office facilities that had reported zero utilization rates could be identified as potential consolidation opportunities, but had not been identified until we pointed out our findings to the official. The 3 other facilities at that location (which were not offices) were marked for demolition.

The second location had 1 facility, and, according to the Public Works official, this facility is 100 percent utilized and the real property record was reported correctly in the Army's General Fund Enterprise Business System. However, the official noted that this facility had two real property unique identifier numbers—reflecting an error in DOD's Real Property Assets Database, which had not been found until we identified it.

The third location had 4 facilities, and, according to the real property officer, 2 of the facilities were put on the installation's demolition list as of February 2014 and the other 2 facilities have usable space that is being considered for reuse by other activities needing space.

OSD and the military departments have taken some steps to make improvements to the completeness and accuracy of their data since 2011; however, based on our analysis of OSD's Real Property Assets Database, there continues to be incomplete and inaccurate data. In September 2011, we recommended that DOD develop and implement a methodology for calculating and recording utilization data for all types of

---

[37]As noted above, we used four data fields—the utilization rate, the status, the property description, and whether the asset was described and reported as "utilized."

GAO-14-538 Defense Infrastructure

facilities, and modify processes to update and verify the accuracy of reported utilization data to reflect a facility's true status. As previously discussed, DOD partially concurred with the recommendation and stated that it recognized the need for further improvements in the collection and reporting of utilization data across the department. Further, DOD stated at the time that it had already begun some efforts to improve utilization data, but it did not specify what actions it had completed to date or the time frames for completing efforts to improve collection and reporting of utilization data. Fully implementing our September 2011 recommendation would help provide reasonable assurance that the utilization data are complete and accurate, which could also help better position the military services to identify consolidation opportunities and realize the potential attendant cost avoidance from no longer maintaining and operating more facility space than needed.

OSD Does Not Have a Strategic Plan to Manage DOD's Real Property Efficiently and Facilitate the Identification of Opportunities for Consolidating Unutilized or Underutilized Facilities

OSD does not have a strategic plan to manage DOD's real property efficiently and facilitate the department in identifying opportunities for consolidating unutilized or underutilized facilities. According to DOD Directive 4165.06,[38] it is DOD policy that DOD real property shall be managed to promote the most efficient and economic use of DOD real property assets and in the most economical manner, consistent with defense requirements. In addition, our prior work has shown that organizations need sound strategic management planning in order to identify and achieve long-range goals and objectives. Our prior work also identified critical elements that should be incorporated into strategic plans to establish a comprehensive, results-oriented management framework. A results-oriented management framework approach includes a strategic plan with, among other things, long-term goals, and strategies to achieve the goals, and metrics or performance measures to gauge progress of the implementation to meet the goals.[39]

While OSD has established a directive and a number of instructions for the management of real property, including for the maintenance of data elements about their facilities, OSD has not developed a strategic plan nor established department-wide goals, strategies to achieve the goals, or

---

[38]Department of Defense Directive 4165.06, *Real Property* (Oct. 13, 2004, certified current Nov. 18, 2008).

[39]GAO-09-865; GAO-10-526; and GAO-10-585.

metrics to gauge progress for how it intends to manage its real property in the most economical and efficient manner. Two critical elements of a strategic plan are the establishment of long-term goals and a description of strategies to achieve those goals. Such goals could be focused on correcting inaccurate and incomplete facility utilization-rate data in OSD's Real Property Assets Database to provide better visibility on the status of the utilized, unutilized, and underutilized facilities. Another goal could be to identify opportunities for consolidating unutilized or underutilized facilities in order to effectively and efficiently use facilities as well as to reduce operation and maintenance costs in a time of declining defense budgets. Further, OSD has not established department-wide metrics for assessing progress related to real property management. Such metrics could be used to gauge progress in the efficient utilization of DOD's current real property inventory. For example, a metric could be established for the military departments to complete a 100 percent inventory of all their real property at their respective installations within a specific time frame in order to baseline the number of utilized, unutilized, and underutilized facilities, which could help them to identify consolidation opportunities. OSD officials acknowledged that there is currently no OSD strategic plan that clearly establishes long-term goals, strategies to achieve the goals, and the use of metrics to gauge progress to manage DOD's real property, because DOD has focused on other priorities. However, real property management is a long-standing issue and DOD's real property assets represent significant resources, as well as the opportunity for cost savings through the consolidation or disposal of unutilized or underutilized inventory. Without a strategic plan that includes long-term goals, strategies to achieve the goals, and metrics to gauge progress, it will be difficult for OSD to effectively manage its facilities, and it may be missing opportunities to identify additional consolidation opportunities, and therefore may not be utilizing its facilities to their utmost extent.

Conclusions

OSD has made some progress in improving the completeness and accuracy of its facility utilization data in its Real Property Assets Database. However, there continues to be incomplete and inaccurate data at the OSD and military-service level. We continue to believe that fully implementing our 2011 recommendation to develop and implement a methodology for calculating and recording utilization data for all types of facilities, and to modify processes to update and verify the accuracy of reported utilization data to reflect a facility's true status, would help provide reasonable assurance that the utilization data are complete and accurate. Further, OSD's lack of a strategic plan to facilitate the department's management of its real property puts OSD and the military departments at risk for missing consolidation opportunities. As part of a results-oriented management framework, such a strategic plan should contain, among other things, long-term goals; strategies to achieve the goals; and the use of metrics to gauge progress. Without an OSD strategic plan, OSD and the military departments will be challenged in managing their real property in an efficient and economical manner, as required, and in identifying utilized, unutilized, or underutilized facilities as well as consolidation opportunities.

Recommendation for Executive Action

To better enable DOD to manage its real property inventory effectively and efficiently, we recommend that the Secretary of Defense direct the Deputy Under Secretary of Defense for Installations and Environment to establish a strategic plan as part of a results-oriented management framework that includes, among other things, long-term goals, strategies to achieve the goals, and use of metrics to gauge progress to manage DOD's real property and to facilitate DOD's ability to identify all unutilized or underutilized facilities for potential consolidation opportunities.

Agency Comments

We provided a draft of this report to DOD for official review and comment. In its comments, DOD concurred with our recommendation and stated that a strategy review is currently underway with initial guidance and initiatives to be identified by the close of the calendar year. DOD also provided technical comments which we incorporated in our report as appropriate. DOD's written comments are reproduced in their entirety in appendix III.

We are sending copies of this report to the appropriate congressional committees; the Secretary of Defense; Deputy Under Secretary of Defense for Installations and Environment; the Secretaries of the Army, Navy, and Air Force; the Commandant of the Marine Corps; and the Director, Office of Management and Budget. In addition, the report is available at no charge on the GAO website at http://www.gao.gov.

If you or your staff have any questions about this report, please contact me at (202) 512-4523 or leporeb@gao.gov. Contact points for our Offices of Congressional Relations and Public Affairs may be found on the last page of this report. GAO staff who made key contributions to this report are listed in appendix IV.

Brian J. Lepore
Director
Defense Capabilities and Management

List of Committees

The Honorable Carl Levin
Chairman
The Honorable James M. Inhofe
Ranking Member
Committee on Armed Services
United States Senate

The Honorable Richard J. Durbin
Chairman
The Honorable Thad Cochran
Ranking Member
Subcommittee on Defense
Committee on Appropriations
United States Senate

The Honorable Tim Johnson
Chairman
The Honorable Mark Kirk
Ranking Member
Subcommittee on Military Construction, Veterans' Affairs,
   and Related Agencies
Committee on Appropriations
United States Senate

The Honorable Howard P. "Buck" McKeon
Chairman
The Honorable Adam Smith
Ranking Member
Committee on Armed Services
House of Representatives

The Honorable Rodney Frelinghuysen
Chairman
The Honorable Pete Visclosky
Ranking Member
Subcommittee on Defense
Committee on Appropriations
House of Representatives

The Honorable John Culberson
Chairman
The Honorable Sanford Bishop, Jr.
Ranking Member
Subcommittee on Military Construction, Veterans Affairs,
    and Related Agencies
Committee on Appropriations
House of Representatives

Appendix I: Scope and Methodology

To determine the extent to which the Office of the Secretary of Defense (OSD) has improved the completeness and accuracy of facility utilization data in its Real Property Assets Database and the military services use the data contained in their respective real property inventory databases to identify potential consolidation opportunities, we obtained selected data fields containing the military services' real property records from OSD's Real Property Assets Database. We selected the same data fields we had used as part of our methodology and analysis for our September 2011 report.[1] Specifically, we analyzed the utilization-rate data fields for fiscal years 2010 through 2013—the most recent full year available at the time of this review—to determine whether more complete utilization-rate data had been entered since our previous review of the fiscal year 2010 data. We assessed the reliability of the Department of Defense's (DOD) real property inventory data by (1) performing electronic testing for obvious errors in accuracy and completeness, (2) reviewing existing information about the data and the system that produced them, and (3) interviewing agency officials knowledgeable about the data. We determined that the data were sufficiently reliable to assess the trends of the utilization data reported in OSD's Real Property Assets Database for fiscal years 2010 through 2013. We also reviewed our prior work on excess and underutilized real property to understand issues previously identified with real property management. We gathered and analyzed documentation, such as a DOD directive and instructions as well as military department regulations, reflecting OSD's and the military departments' management of real property and how OSD used the data contained in its Real Property Assets Database to identify unutilized or underutilized facilities or potential consolidation opportunities. We interviewed officials in the Office of the Under Secretary of Defense for Installations & Environment; each of the three military departments, which include the four military services; and the military service installations we visited, and discussed their processes to manage real property. We selected 11 active military installations to visit to include installations from the four services and to reflect those with high numbers of buildings.[2] While the results of our interviews and visits cannot be generalized to all

---

[1] GAO-11-814.

[2] For our methodology, we selected 11 active installations that each had at least 500 buildings on them as reported in *OSD's Base Structure Report Fiscal Year 2013 Baseline*. The selection included 3 Army, 3 Navy, 2 Marine Corps, and 3 Air Force installations or bases, which represented 5.4 percent of the 203 active installations and bases within the continental United States excluding the National Guard and the Reserves.

installations, they provided perspectives on how installations manage their real property. Using OSD's Real Property Assets Database and the following data fields—the utilization rate, the status as "active," and the property description as "building," we used a fourth data field, which described the asset as "utilized," to determine any inconsistencies that might exist between these data fields. Using these four criteria, we reviewed the real property records for the 11 installations we visited to identify the extent to which other consolidation opportunities, if any, may exist on the installations and potential inconsistencies and inaccuracies. We contacted and received information from DOD representatives, as delineated in table 6.

Table 6: DOD Offices and Installations Contacted during GAO's Review

Office of the Secretary of Defense	Office of the Under Secretary of Defense for Installations and Environment, Virginia
Army	• Office of the Assistant Chief of Staff for Installation Management, Virginia
	• Fort Bragg, North Carolina
	• Fort Carson, Colorado
	• Joint Base Lewis McChord, Washington
Navy	• Commander, Navy Installations Command Headquarters, Virginia
	• Navy Region Mid-Atlantic, Virginia
	• Naval Station Norfolk, Virginia
	• Naval Base Coronado, California
	• Naval Base Kitsap, Washington
Marine Corps	• Headquarters Marine Corps, Virginia
	• Camp Pendleton, California
	• Camp Lejeune, North Carolina
Air Force	• Headquarters Air Force, Asset Management and Operations Division, Virginia
	• Minot Air Force Base, North Dakota
	• Eglin Air Force Base, Florida
	• Vandenberg Air Force Base, California

Source: GAO. I GAO-14-538

To determine the extent to which OSD has a strategic plan to manage DOD's real property efficiently and to facilitate the identification of unutilized and underutilized facilities, we obtained and analyzed documentation, such as the Office of the Deputy Under Secretary of Defense for Installations and Environment report, *2013 Accomplishments and 2014 Goals and Objectives*, a DOD directive and instructions, and military department regulations for the management of real property. We also reviewed OSD's Real Property Assets Database as of September 30, 2013—the most recent data available at the time of our review—to identify what facilities, if any, were reported as being unutilized or underutilized and ascertain how OSD implemented its policy and guidance to manage real property in the most economical manner. We discussed the policies and guidance used in managing these facilities with officials in the Office of the Under Secretary of Defense for Installations & Environment and compared OSD's efforts and guidance to the DOD directive and instructions for real property management and the results-oriented management framework as a best practice for strategic planning.[3]

We conducted this performance audit from July 2013 to September 2014 in accordance with generally accepted government auditing standards. Those standards require that we plan and perform the audit to obtain sufficient, appropriate evidence to provide a reasonable basis for our findings and conclusions based on our audit objectives. We believe that

---

[3]Department of Defense Directive 4165.06, *Real Property* (Oct. 13, 2004, certified current Nov.18, 2008); Department of Defense Instruction 4165.70, *Real Property Management* (Apr. 6, 2005); and Department of Defense Instruction 4165.14, *Real Property Inventory (RPI) and Forecasting* (Jan. 17, 2014). See, for example, GAO, *Managing for Results: Critical Issues for Improving Federal Agencies' Strategic Plans*, GAO/GGD-97-180 (Washington, D.C.: Sept .16, 1997); *Major Management Challenges and Program Risks: A Governmentwide Perspective*, GAO-03-95 (Washington, D.C.: January 2003); and *Military Transformation: Clear Leadership, Accountability, and Management Tools Are Needed to Enhance DOD's Efforts to Transform Military Capabilities*, GAO-05-70 (Washington, D.C.: Dec. 17, 2004). These reports described that strategic plans are the starting point and basic underpinning for results-oriented management, a results-oriented management framework can help the federal government operate effectively, and successful organizations in both the public and private sectors use results-oriented management tools to help achieve desired program outcomes. One of the reports identified the framework that includes various management tools, such as long-term goals, strategies to be used, performance goals, and performance measures, among others. To determine these best practices, we found studies by several organizations, including us, that show that results-oriented management tools or principles, derived from the Government Performance and Results Act of 1993, provide agencies with a management framework for effectively implementing and managing programs and shift program management focus from measuring program activities and processes to measuring program outcomes. See GAO, *Results-Oriented Government: GPRA Has Established a Solid Foundation for Achieving Greater Results*, GAO-04-38 (Washington, D.C.: Mar. 10, 2004); *Managing For Results: Enhancing Agency Use of Performance Information for Management Decision Making*, GAO-05-927 (Washington, D.C.: Sept. 9, 2005); and *Results-Oriented Management: Strengthening Key Practices at FEMA and Interior Could Promote Greater Use of Performance Information*, GAO-09-676 (Washington, D.C.: Aug. 17, 2009) for additional details on the methodology used to determine these best practices.

GAO-14-538 Defense Infrastructure

the evidence obtained provides a reasonable basis for our findings and conclusions based on our audit objectives.

Appendix II: Key DOD and Military Department Real Property Guidance and Excerpts of the Requirements

The Department of Defense's (DOD) Real Property Management Program is governed by statute[1] and DOD regulations, directives, and instructions that establish real property accountability and financial reporting requirements. Table 7 describes some of the guidance from DOD and the military departments and includes excerpts of the related requirements to manage real property.

Table 7: Key DOD and Military Department Real Property Guidance and Excerpts of the Requirements

DOD and military department guidance	Excerpts of the requirements
DOD Financial Management Regulation 7000.14-R, Volume 4, Chapter 6, *Property, Plant, and Equipment* (June 2009)	States that entries to record financial transactions in accounting-system general ledger accounts and the supporting subsidiary property-accountability records and systems must, among other things, enable periodic, independent verification of the accuracy of the accounting and accountability records through periodic physical counts or inventories, or both, of property, plant, and equipment for existence and completeness.
	Requires DOD components to perform a physical inventory of general real property at least every 5 years. Real property Heritage Assets must be inventoried at least every 3 years.
DOD Directive 4165.06, *Real Property* (Oct. 13, 2004, certified current Nov. 18, 2008)	States that it is DOD policy that, in accordance with Executive Order 13327, DOD real property shall be managed to promote the most efficient and economic use of DOD real property assets and to ensure management accountability for implementing federal real property reforms.
	Assigns overall responsibility and oversight to the Under Secretary of Defense for Acquisition, Technology and Logistics of DOD real property and requires the Under Secretary to establish overarching guidance and procedures for the acquisition, management, and disposal of DOD real property.
	Requires the Secretaries of the military departments to implement policies and programs to acquire, manage, and dispose of real property in accordance with this directive. Those policies and programs shall ensure that their military departments establish and maintain an accurate inventory to account for the real property under the departments' management; and budget and financially manage to meet the real property requirements applicable to their departments.

[1] Section 2721 of Title 10 of the United States Code directs the Secretary of Defense to prescribe regulations to, among other things, have the records of fixed property of the military departments maintained on a quantitative and monetary basis, to the extent practicable.

DOD and military department guidance	Excerpts of the requirements
DOD Instruction 4165.70, *Real Property Management*, (Apr. 6, 2005)	Assigns responsibility to the Deputy Under Secretary of Defense for Installations and Environment for providing additional guidance and procedures, as required, for implementing real property management policy.
	Requires the Secretaries of the military departments to establish programs and procedures to manage real property in accordance with applicable law and certain policies, procedures, and guidance. They are also required to accurately inventory and account for the real property under their accountability, and maintain a program monitoring the use of real property to ensure that all real property holdings under their control are being used to the maximum extent possible consistent with both peacetime and mobilization requirements.
	Assigns responsibility to real property administrators within the military departments for maintaining a current inventory and up-to-date information regarding the cost, functional use, status, condition, utilization, present value, maintenance and management of each individual real property unit in their real property inventory, among other things.
	Requires DOD components (including military departments) to periodically review[a] their real property holdings, both land and facilities, to identify unneeded and underused property.
DOD Instruction 4165.14, *Real Property Inventory (RPI) and Forecasting*, (Jan. 17, 2014)	Provides general procedures for reporting the required information during the acquisition, management, and disposal of a real property asset to maintain a complete and accurate real property inventory and the Real Property Information Model data that must be verified in the physical inventory process.
	Requires the military departments and the Washington Headquarters Services, among other things, to report changes observed since the prior physical inventories, which occur every 5 years or, for those real property assets designated as historic, every 3 years; ensure their real property inventory is accurate and auditable; certify that the real property inventory has been reconciled; and verify and validate minimum asset information for each DOD facility, including the utilization rate during a physical inventory.
Army Regulation 405-70, *Utilization of Real Property* (May 12, 2006)	Establishes planning and management procedures to ensure efficient use of Army real property and requires installation commanders to conduct an annual real property utilization survey of each assigned installation, subinstallation, or facility. The utilization survey reports contain findings of unused, underutilized, or excess real property.
Naval Facilities Engineering Command P-78, *Real Property Inventory (RPI) Procedures Manual* (July 2012)	Provides the responsibilities and procedures for managing Department of Navy (comprising the Navy and the Marine Corps) Real Property Inventory information. It covers the organizational responsibilities for real property and the Internet Navy Facility Assets Data Store Management System, which is the official record of the Navy's and Marine Corps' real property assets.
Air Force Policy Directive 32-90, *Real Property Asset Management* (Aug. 6, 2007)	States that the Air Force will accurately manage its real property asset inventory while efficiently and effectively sustaining its inventory in accordance with Federal Real Property Council guidance. States that the intent of Air Force real property asset management is to sustain real property assets at the right size, cost, and condition to accomplish Air Force missions and objectives. States that, to maximize efficiency of its operations, the Air Force will continually assess its real property asset portfolio against ongoing and projected mission needs, and use a systematic approach to determine whether retaining property assets provides the best value to the Air Force.
Air Force Policy Directive 32-10, *Installations and Facilities* (Mar. 4, 2010)	Provides for the responsibilities and authorities, including assigning the Air Force Civil Engineer to formulate specific operational and procedural guidance to implement broad policy, to advocate for resources, to oversee execution of installations and facilities programs, and to develop and manage common levels of service in cooperation with the Under Secretary of Defense for Acquisition, Technology and Logistics.

Source: GAO analysis of DOD and military service data. | GAO-14-538

[a]This DOD instruction does not specify the time intervals for periodic review, but the Army requires an annual utilization survey.

Appendix III: Comments from the Department of Defense

OFFICE OF THE UNDER SECRETARY OF DEFENSE
3000 DEFENSE PENTAGON
WASHINGTON, DC 20301-3000

ACQUISITION,
TECHNOLOGY,
AND LOGISTICS

AUG 2 2 2014

Mr. Brian J. Lepore
Director, Defense Capabilities and Management
U.S. Government Accountability Office
441 G Street, NW
Washington, D.C. 20548

Dear Mr. Lepore:

This is the Department of Defense (DoD) response to the Draft Report GAO-14-538, "DEFENSE INFRASTRUCTURE: DoD Needs to Improve its Efforts to Identify Unutilized and Underutilized Facilities," dated July 24, 2014 (GAO Code 351841). Comments on the report recommendation are enclosed.

Thank you for the opportunity to comment on the draft report. Should you have questions, please contact Mr. Bob Coffman, (571)372-6840, robert.a.coffman10.civ@mail.mil.

Sincerely,

John Conger
Acting Deputy Undersecretary of Defense
Installations and Environment

Enclosure:
As stated

GAO DRAFT REPORT DATED JULY 24, 2014
GAO-14-538 (GAO CODE 351841)

"DEFENSE INFRASTRUCTURE: DOD NEEDS TO IMPROVE ITS EFFORTS TO
IDENTIFY UNUTILIZED AND UNDERUTILIZED FACILITIES"

DEPARTMENT OF DEFENSE COMMENTS
TO THE GAO RECOMMENDATION

RECOMMENDATION: To better enable DOD to manage its real property inventory
effectively and efficiently, we recommend that the Secretary of Defense direct the Deputy Under
Secretary of Defense for Installations and Environment to establish a strategic plan as part of a
results-oriented management framework, which includes, among others, long-term goals,
strategies to achieve the goals, and use of metrics to gauge progress to manage DOD's real
property to facilitate DOD's ability to identify all unutilized or underutilized facilities for
potential consolidation opportunities.

DoD RESPONSE: Concur. A strategy and policy review is currently underway, with initial
guidance and initiatives to be identified by the close of the calendar year. The outcome of this
effort will bolster and guide the Department's efforts in achieving a reasonable level of
performance from its diverse real property portfolio as the Department adjusts to the dwindling
resources and increasing excess capacity that result from the new force structure and Defense
Strategy.

Through the continuing efforts of the Military Services to achieve a sustainable state of audit
readiness by June of 2016, key business processes and internal controls are under review with
gaps and weaknesses addressed through corrective action plans. The positive results of
corrective actions should be reflected in the increased accuracy and confidence of the real
property inventory information. The process for physical inventory is among those to be
reviewed, and utilization rate is among those key financial statement and management and
budget data that must be verified in the physical inventory of real property. This requirement is
documented in the November 2013 version of the DoD Financial Improvement and Audit
Readiness Guidance, as well as in Department of Defense Instruction 4165.14, *Real Property
Inventory and Forecasting,* dated January 17, 2014.

Space management is foundational to proper utilization and is recognized by each of the Military
Departments as a priority in their overall installation and asset management efforts. To that end,
each of the Military Departments are refining or pursuing information technology solutions that
provide a look at the interior of buildings in order to improve the visibility of the type and
amount of space designated for specific purposes, as well as the use and users of those spaces.
This increased awareness of each facility will inform consolidation and assignment
opportunities. This office will continue to monitor the efforts of the Military Departments
through our oversight responsibilities for information technology investments.

Appendix IV: GAO Contact and Staff Acknowledgments

GAO Contact	Brian J. Lepore, (202) 512-4523 or leporeb@gao.gov
Staff Acknowledgments	In addition to the contact named above, Harold Reich (Assistant Director), James Ashley, Ronnie Bergman, Pat Bohan, Tracy Burney, Cynthia Grant, Mary Catherine Hult, Cheryl Weissman, and Michael Willems made key contributions to this report.

GAO's Mission	The Government Accountability Office, the audit, evaluation, and investigative arm of Congress, exists to support Congress in meeting its constitutional responsibilities and to help improve the performance and accountability of the federal government for the American people. GAO examines the use of public funds; evaluates federal programs and policies; and provides analyses, recommendations, and other assistance to help Congress make informed oversight, policy, and funding decisions. GAO's commitment to good government is reflected in its core values of accountability, integrity, and reliability.
Obtaining Copies of GAO Reports and Testimony	The fastest and easiest way to obtain copies of GAO documents at no cost is through GAO's website (http://www.gao.gov). Each weekday afternoon, GAO posts on its website newly released reports, testimony, and correspondence. To have GAO e-mail you a list of newly posted products, go to http://www.gao.gov and select "E-mail Updates."
Order by Phone	The price of each GAO publication reflects GAO's actual cost of production and distribution and depends on the number of pages in the publication and whether the publication is printed in color or black and white. Pricing and ordering information is posted on GAO's website, http://www.gao.gov/ordering.htm. Place orders by calling (202) 512-6000, toll free (866) 801-7077, or TDD (202) 512-2537. Orders may be paid for using American Express, Discover Card, MasterCard, Visa, check, or money order. Call for additional information.
Connect with GAO	Connect with GAO on Facebook, Flickr, Twitter, and YouTube. Subscribe to our RSS Feeds or E-mail Updates. Listen to our Podcasts. Visit GAO on the web at www.gao.gov.
To Report Fraud, Waste, and Abuse in Federal Programs	Contact: Website: http://www.gao.gov/fraudnet/fraudnet.htm E-mail: fraudnet@gao.gov Automated answering system: (800) 424-5454 or (202) 512-7470
Congressional Relations	Katherine Siggerud, Managing Director, siggerudk@gao.gov, (202) 512-4400, U.S. Government Accountability Office, 441 G Street NW, Room 7125, Washington, DC 20548
Public Affairs	Chuck Young, Managing Director, youngc1@gao.gov, (202) 512-4800 U.S. Government Accountability Office, 441 G Street NW, Room 7149 Washington, DC 20548